INSIDE OUT

WORDS CARRYING MY FEELINGS.

DR. SHRADDHA S. BELOSE PITALE

This book is dedicated to all the beautiful Souls who have either been told they are wonderful or told they're not.

Contents

Foreword

'INSIDE OUT, Words Carrying My Feelings' is a creative poetry work done by my beloved sister (a doctor by profession), who can now be addressed as a poetess. She started her journey of writing long back in her teenage and still continues to write. She is a stern believer in a holistic approach to treatment and hence she also finds magic in those lucid words carrying vivid feelings, to create and fetch vibes to herself and her readers.

Apart from her work in English, she is well appreciated for her 'quote writing and poetries' in Hindi and Marathi languages as well. Having a dream to write and publish a book someday, she has now made her way to this beautiful compilation of her poetries in her first-ever book 'Inside Out'. Wherein this book brings to you the platter of poetries in its pristine form as playful, placid, praiseworthy, perky and picturesque as she once ago penned it.

Talking about the poetry work in this book, one can see that poetess has deliberately taken the opportunity to picture her feelings and her experiences from her till-now life. Also adding some imaginary sequences and fictional characters to her creative writing, she has given poetries a unique touch. One can easily relate to the life situations described through these poetries. Moreover, you can find love, love relationship, a life of a teen entering adulthood, passion and compassion in life, miseries, strengths, etc on which the gist of each poetry is based.

This is a proud moment for her and her loved ones (including me) as she has stepped into this new expedition of book writing. Hope you all find her poetry work interesting and heart-warming. Hope you all enjoy reading!

- Shreya Gosavi

(Nutritionist and a Reader)

Preface

It gives me immense pleasure to bring this book of poetry to light for readers now which was otherwise limited to my own muse.

All the poetries written in this book are a good blend of three things- my life experiences, my feelings and my creative thinking and writing upon it. As each of these poetries is written at different times and in different moods and mental states, one can feel that reading all at once can give you mixed feelings, not the point of concern though. But reading each piece of poetry as a single story will rather give you a deeper comprehensive experience and can create for you the sentimental value regardless of what I had felt in the same scenario.

I must say 'Writing' has got me thinking about doing well in life directly or indirectly by means of understanding something, decluttering my mind or simply relishing something good that happened. Having a dream of publishing a book someday was one of the key motivations for my writing work.

Each of the poems definitely carries a piece of my heart then giving me the courage to write another one wholeheartedly. Hope you all enjoy reading each of them.

Thank You!

Dr. Shraddha S. Belose Pitale

Acknowledgements

For my dream of writing a book, I'm extremely grateful to all those who have inspired me directly or indirectly through their words, thoughts or actions.

This project would not have been possible without the direct support of my beloved parents, my loving husband and my siblings who undoubtedly let me explore and grow my talent in various fields.

I'd like to express my deepest thanks to my closest friends who always have my back and backed me with their motivation, assistance, presence, and precious time as and when I needed them the most.

I can't thank God enough for all the strength and blessings bestowed upon me.

Last but not least, thanks to all my readers who like my work and had appreciated me timely. Thank you, everyone!

1. LIFE

Life is One,
So do not try to Shun.
Embrace as it Comes.
Believe! It will be the greatest Fun.
Life is the Rain,
So do not let it go in Vain.
Make it best as you Gain.
Cause no pleasures without Pain.
Life is a Run,
Full of Twists and Turns.
Give a damn! You will definitely Learn.
Something to lose and more to Earn.
Life is a Ray,
Though small will lead your Way.
Along with you till the last Day.
Worth living! You will Say.
#SS22
#myfirstpoetry

2. WANT TO LIVE

Every second passes by,
On the green lawn, I still lie.
A cool breeze to fondle, looking at the sky.
Pondering how in this huge world I just fit?
So want to live full of it.
Every minute I give a thought,
In my jigsaw puzzle, I get caught.
Let's play smart, cause life is short.
Do not want to miss a single bit,
So want to live full of it.
Every then is the next day,
But tomorrow will become a today.
Getting no sore, I smile wide to stay.
Many things I know I could meet,
So want to live full of it.
#SS22

3. BEAUTY THROUGH BEAST

Rusted brain, stagnant heart,
from beauty, you turned to a beast.
Grimful eyes, frozen hands,
A nightmare you never expected even at least.
From shameful, you turned shameless.
You doubt yourself while clearing this mess.
Sunken down with all regrets,
Amidst the chaos, completely helpless.
Look how ugly, horrid, frightful, awful you!
Don't be afraid.
You are a son of the Almighty!
Thrown deeper down the dale,
To realize heaven through hell.
So for every night-fall, you learn to stand tall.
March ahead, surpass the darkest wall.
Again from the beast, you will be the beauty,
Cause you are a son of the Almighty.
#SS22

4. VINTAGE WOE

Shattered and scattered, already broken, you came to me.
With cold hands and a numb mind, hoping to seek.
I tried far to soak all your blues,
Cause I was a blank page with no clues.
Wise men told me, I will get hurt to your broken edge.
For I was a new spring to your dull Vintage.
It was a hard long leap,
But I FELL (fall in love) and managed to grip.
Then you backed off, for there was not enough mend.
Accepting it so hard, I stopped and I went.
This was our story with an endless end.
#SS22

5. HAPPY PARTING BE LIKE

"We were never meant to be....."
Say with no absolute regrets.
Still sharing
Same land and same air.
Cause for ourselves, we always care.
No matter,
We will always smile.
Cause in our heavenly body dwells a sweet little child!
#SS22

6. HER MOONLIGHT

She dreamt of her Big day...
Dressed in White.
Mistakenly happy in...
Being slaved and Tight.
It was all love...
Yes, Love that is barely Right?
Stuck in the daylight...
Gloomy Bright!
Illusionary Sun...
Scared her Tonight.
Sooner or later just...
She escaped in her Moonlight!
#SS22

7. IN LOVELY SILENCE

Understanding Herself to Know Him better,
was the thing SHE Believed.
Knowing Her to Understand Himself better,
was the way HE Relived.
While World Wondered Who Was Selfish among Two!
The Two had already known the Magic of BALANCE,
In lovely Silence!
#SS22

8. LET IT OOZE

For they were the ones who Suffered,
But they did not Die.
The vulnerability was all at the Top,
But they did Willfully Sigh.
They Believed their Inside,
("stay safely away,") they say now to you.
Why don't they Believe YOU?
Maybe for them, you are the Weaker,
Or they are yet the Unhealed Blue.
("Learn Before you Dive, or Dive to Learn,")
They should say, without keeping you away.
Getting through waters is what a brave one Chooses.
Either Blessings or Lessons to turn.
Feel the Numbness, before some Muse.
Let Your Mind wonder, let it Lose.
Let Your Heart break, let it Ooze.
#SS22

9. FLOWER

How could I see someone else plucking you?
For I never had a thought of even touching your fragile core!
YOU ARE A DELICATELY COLOURFUL FLOWER!
But I could see you now trying hard to become someone's decor!
You are priceless to me.
But you have chosen yourself to be priced!
I believe your beauty was in your unplucked being.
But I see you getting exploited in your own exploring way to entice!
As Life moves ahead at its pace,
I PRAY YOUR FRAGRANCE LAST FOREVER, NOT FOR ME OR THEM, AS YOU MIGHT NEED YOUR OWN 'SOLACE'.
#SS22

10. WAS NEVER EASY

Was never easy to STOP YOU
from Gazing all time at me.
Was never easy to STOP ME
from Falling deep for you.
Was never easy to STOP YOU
from Drifting away from me.
Was never easy to STOP ME
from Waiting hard for you.
Was never easy to STOP US!
#SS22

11. LOVE PERSONIFIED

My PeN is Singing Your sonG!
My LovE in the Air is Dancing for You.
My PageS for You are Running lonG!
Am I the only one Sitting Quite Gazing at You?
Everything Around feels aLive.
Alas! My Love is PersonifieD.
#SS22

12. MY IMMORTAL EMOTIONS

My
Emotions those left Unset with Times,
Are now Here,
settled in my Verses and my Lines.
Maybe safer now,
from being (over) Touched.
Or
Maybe safer now,
from being UnTouched??
I no longer fear it,
from getting Disappeared with passing Time.
I no longer fear,
to keep it Ever Shine.

Cause all I Believe now is to create them all Afresh.
Wherever and Whenever, as they are all Mine!
My
Immortal Emotions they are!
#SS22

13. JUMBLED

I had always let you choose
your own best choice.
Yes I will also let you choose
someone over me!
Cause all I want is happy you,
with dissatisfaction to the least.
But I know you are never settled in mind
when left with many options.
Then I try my best to clear your confusion,
only to get you a better selection.
How can I say now, when for you I'm myself an option
and you need my suggestion?
You are JUMBLED, and so do I.
#SS22

14. TRUE WARRIOR

You Are A True Warrior.
Guarding The Hearts Of Evil,
BUT Fighting Strong Against Evil Minds In Town!
You Are A True Warrior.
Bringing Yourself Up Above Victory,
BUT Putting Not Your Victims Anymore Down!
You Are A True Warrior.
Winning The Battle for Love,
BUT Losing To The Narcissistic Crown!
#SS22

15. OHH, STARS! IT'S MY WILL

Some believe 'them' in the first place and some don't at all.

But I believe 'them' saying, they stand just second after my only true WILL.

I believe in my energy and so do in theirs.

'EM are Stars, who helps those, those who help themselves!

#SS22

#willpower

#star@strology

16. SUN OF YOUR LIFE

It puts you on the pinnacle to shine sometimes.
It burns you sometimes in flame.
It tames you sometimes.
And sometimes leave you untamed.
Sometimes it seems to disappear
when your face is black,
but then you rediscover that it's behind you
always having your back.
It is the SUN of your Life!
#SS22
#majorpersoninlife

17. MOON OF TODAY

The Moon of today
Will make new memories,
Will cherish old for some.
While I sit still to just adore One!
#SS22
#beingselenophile

18. LOST LOVE

I Placed You In My Heart,
You Tucked Me In Your Void.
Replacing Me Was Your Art,
You Just Left Me Paranoid.
Ohh, Lost Love!
#SS22

19. IT'S OFFICIAL

One Day Wasn't So USUAL.
Yet They Pretended To Be CASUAL.
Guess It Was Something MUTUAL.
Which Wasn't Any HABITUAL.
They Wanted To Make It PERPETUAL.
It Was Love In ACTUAL!
Oh So CRUCIAL!
Now It's OFFICIAL!

#SS22
#officiallycouple
#couplelove

20. BLOODY RED! PERIOD

Me and Red.
Day in and Day out.
All the day throughout.
As it goes- one, two, three, four.
On day five, maybe little or nothing to Sore.
The days repeat.
Every month, in a cycle.
The bloody red at its pinnacle.
Maybe a day ahead or a day later.
Sometimes too early or no sooner.
But that is how it is said to Recycle.
The Day Before Day One.
Wanting to do just none.
Look at the mind, still running in haste.
Adding to the madness with twist n turn.
The mood Sswinngss in mere waste.
I need all food to feed my 'no fun'.
But my body knows No taste.
Everything is turning numb.
Yet there is agony in Tender breast.
Oh, that's PMS, I want some Rest!
But words in aches have no voice.
This is how the bloody red makes noise.

Time slows down.
As pain is gearing up.
I am suddenly Wet.
Guess what? it is not the sweat.
By the time my bottoms are heavy,
I reach to figure it out.
It's already soaked into the floral prints on my pant.
Call me mad. But let me Shouttttt!
"you Bloody Red".......PERIOD.

#SS22
#bloodred
#periods

21. HE LOVES HER. PERIOD

"Darling,

❤I know it's painful to your core.

❤Don't worry, I won't hurt you anymore.

❤Let the days pass 1...,2...,3...,4...

❤You'll be healed, We shall make Love even more."

....

Bleeding Red, she went no wild.
Cause this is how he cared and made her smile.

#SS22

#periods

22. ON A FORWARD JOURNEY

Confidence holding my hand right,
Struggles accelerate me now.
Happiness hugging me tight,
Lessons have my back somehow.

Fears are my fellow fierce,
Pains are my booster.
Often wearing smiley tears,
Love guides me to foster.

Memories kiss me at the hardest times,
Kindness kindle a new track.
For a lifetime, words rhyme,
My Soul now is an enriched pack.

#SS22

' My Quote Writing '

- *You Are An Art And An Artist Too!*

- *iLLuminate Beyond iLLusion.*

- *Don't Wish For Simple Life And Later Dump It Saying It's Mediocre. Aim For Richful Life And Keep It Simple.*

- *Keep Your 'Passion Quotient' High In Your Failures And 'Compassion Quotient' High In Your Victories.*

- *Because When the Rest Of Them Only Found Best In Him, Only She Found Best In The Rest Of Him!*

- *Not Every Fake Smile Will Destroy You, Some Will Fake Smile To Save You From Being Destroyed.*

- *Not Every Wall Around You Need To Be Broken*

Completely, In An Obscure Pursuit Of Freedom. Do Not Unroof Yourself. You Aren't Caged, Just Mis-Protected. All You Need Is To Get Ventilated Good Enough!

•

And Sometimes You Need An Escape 'To Forget Who You Are' And 'To Know Who You Are' At The Same Time.

•

Universe Will Help You If You Help Yourself To Help Others.

For more quotes and poetries in English, Hindi and Marathi, do follow My Instagram handle:

shraddha_swastik22

My Email:

shraddha22belose@gmail.com

-Dr. Shraddha S. Belose Pitale

THANK YOU FOR READING.

Printed by Libri Plureos GmbH in Hamburg,
Germany